The Prince and Princess of Wales'
WEDDING DAY

On 29 July in the year 1981 His Royal Highness Charles Philip Arthur George, Prince of the United Kingdom of Great Britain and Northern Ireland, Prince of Wales and Earl of Chester, Duke of Cornwall, Duke of Rothesay, Earl of Carrick and Baron of Renfrew, Lord of the Isles and Great Steward of Scotland, eldest son of Her Majesty The Queen and His Royal Highness The Prince Philip, Duke of Edinburgh, was married in St Paul's Cathedral to the Lady Diana Frances Spencer, youngest daughter of the Earl Spencer and the Honourable Mrs Shand Kydd. This is a visual record of that memorable and splendid day in British royal history, produced by Pitkin who have published illustrated books on the great royal occasions ever since *Princess Elizabeth's Wedding Day* in 1947.

'This most memorable and glorious day'

by Peter Lewis

The most popular girl in Britain was marrying the most eligible bachelor and the result was the most glorious and unforgettable day in royal history. It was also the biggest media event of our time. Whether you call it a morale-booster or a lavish piece of escapism, Britain needed it. But so, it appears, did the Americans and the Japanese; around the globe 750 million people, from Mexico to Mauritius, from Bahrain to Brunei, were clamouring to watch.

Their eyes were on the two miles between Buckingham Palace and St Paul's Cathedral, not only because we, the British, were providing what we are indisputably best at – royal pageantry – but because we had something else the world wanted, a love story of a prince and a princess. The atmosphere in the capital built up to a climax the night before, when half a million people turned out with the Royal Family and most of the 'royals' of Europe to watch the fireworks in Hyde Park. The sky was rent with shooting stars but the scene on the ground was just as extraordinary: an atmosphere of carnival had taken over London. People were jamming the streets and many of them were simply refusing to go home.

On a sultry July night they slept on the grass, or jumped in the fountains, or danced in the streets, or settled down with camp chair and thermos flask (and transistor radio or portable television) to wait for the morning.

Dawn stirred the sleepers in the royal parks with the promise of a warm and golden day, a rarity in the summer of 1981. Along the route there was the crunch of empty cans underfoot and overhead the purr of an airship observing the scene with cameras.

Red, white and blue were everywhere – on flags and hats, on bunting and placards, dyeing people's hair and even painting the faces of fanatical patriots. The notable thing was how young the crowd was: the very generation – the under-30s – that might have shrugged off the charisma of royalty was in the front row to pay homage. But then they were there to watch a 20-year-old girl marry into it. These great multi-coloured hedges of people were once again as gentle as British crowds have traditionally been. There were 5,000 uniformed police and hundreds more in plain clothes watching out for trouble. For the first time in our history they lined the route facing the crowd. To our great relief – and theirs – they watched in vain.

Police marksmen on roofs, sniffer dogs on the ground, helicopters in the air – none of them was needed. The only arrests along the route were of a few pickpockets. The police and the crowds were, once again, on the friendliest terms. It was all thanks to the existence of a girl called Diana.

As the sun warmed the sanded roads and the smell of horses and harness that permeates royal pageantry rose in the air, the crowds cheered everything that passed – men watering flowers or sweeping up behind the horses, cars full of guests in hats, bound for the Cathedral. There were home-grown entertainers, like Mr Spike Milligan, who solicited contributions from the crowd in his unaccustomed grey top-hat. There were foreign dignitaries like Mrs Nancy Reagan, wife of the President of the United States, elegant and bandbox-fresh in peach, Princess Grace of Monaco and her son Prince Albert, or the 25-stone King of Tonga, who had installed a specially sturdy seat in the Cathedral.

Then came the carriage processions of our own Royal Family: The Queen in aquamarine, the Queen Mother in eau-de-Nil, Princess Margaret in azalea-peach, Princess Anne in white with a sunflower-burst of a hat.

Finally, from the Palace, came Prince Charles, a slightly tense-looking bridegroom, accompanied by his slightly

LEFT: *The royal fireworks in Hyde Park on the eve of the wedding attracted more than half a million people. At 10pm Prince Charles lighted a beacon which was the signal to start a chain of 101 beacons throughout the British Isles. The 12,000 fireworks were set off to music, culminating in a 35-foot Catherine wheel inscribed with 'VIVAT' and the monograms C and D.*

FACING PAGE: *The first sight of the bride's 25-foot train cascading down the red-carpeted steps beneath Wren's majestic portico. Above it, to the left of the pediment, stands a sign of the times – a lone police sharpshooter.*

ABOVE: *On the way to the Cathedral, The Queen and Prince Philip in their open Semi-State Postillion Landau, surrounded by the panoply of a Sovereign's Escort of Household Cavalry. Theirs was the first of eight carriages in The Queen's procession.*

RIGHT: *In the second carriage rode Queen Elizabeth, the Queen Mother, with the bridegroom's youngest brother, Prince Edward. At 17, he was taking part in his first major royal occasion as one of his brother's 'supporters'.*

FACING PAGE: *Naval salutes from Prince Charles and his 21-year-old midshipman brother, Prince Andrew, as their landau passes the guard of honour on its way out of the Palace. This State Landau was made in 1902 for King Edward VII's coronation. Riding on the back of it in 1981 was an armed detective sergeant (left) disguised in the livery of a footman.*

tense-looking midshipman brother, Prince Andrew, and a lucky silver horseshoe pinned to the red plush interior of their 1902 State Landau, which also bore King Edward VII to his coronation.

The bridegroom, in full dress naval uniform, waved a white-gloved hand, but pulled one of his faint grimaces that indicated tension: understandable, for one of the footmen riding on the carriage was a police bodyguard in disguise.

Then, from out of Clarence House, came the coach everyone was waiting for, the Glass Coach carrying the bride towards her moment of transformation from a Lady into a Princess. Though the coach was 'glass', she was almost invisible behind a cloud of tulle veil, kept in place by the sparkling family tiara of the Spencers. Beside her rode her father, Earl Spencer, beaming with pleasure and pride, determined to enjoy his great day, having attended, in spite of poor health, every rehearsal of the preceding weeks.

Even so, the bridegroom had unfair advantages. He was going to be married surrounded not only by his family by the carriageful, but by the crowned heads of Europe and their consorts, and

other people important in his life, his nanny, his favourite Goons and his trainer's stable lads, his college bed-maker from Cambridge, the prep. school headmaster from Cheam (who once beat him for ragging in the dorm), and a host of friends, helpers and retainers.

But what of Diana? Supported by her two sisters, Jane and Sarah, and her mother, Mrs Shand Kydd, as well as the Earl Spencer, and her former flat-mates and fellow teachers at the Young England Kindergarten, she could be forgiven for feeling very vulnerable.

'I am looking forward', she had told us on television, 'to being a good wife.' All the same, it was a formidable family she was joining in that capacity, a family that filled eight carriages ahead of her on the road, surrounded by the nodding plumes of their escort of Household Cavalry.

She was adding a new name to that awesome family tree – Diana. Now she had to find a new style of being a princess to go with it. After all, her immediate predecessor as Princess of Wales, Queen Mary, relinquished the title 70 years ago; 70 years of such change and upheaval that it might have been 700. She has still to discover what

people expect of a modern Princess of Wales.

But she has made a popular and auspicious start. Already her looks, her hairstyle, her delightful taste in clothes, are serving as models for countless thousands of girls throughout the country. Already she has learned what it means to have, as Prince Charles put it, 'every twitch' scrutinized and re-corded through a battery of lenses. Could she get used to it? 'Just', she said with feeling. In that sense, her glass coach was symbolic. She will be riding in one, on unrelenting display, for the rest of her life.

So the Glass Coach went on its way towards Lady Diana's destiny under Sir Christopher Wren's awe-inspiring dome. She thought Charles was 'pretty amazing' when she first met him. He was 'amazed she's been brave enough to take me on'. Now they were to be amazed together by the experience in store for them – a foretaste of which was 100,000 letters of congratulation and uncounted sacks of presents still stacked in Palace corridors.

But though he was bringing so much to her, so many titles, the landlordship of such varied places as King Arthur's Castle of Tintagel, Dartmoor Prison

Continued on page 8

5

A crowd of 600,000 lined the two-mile route from Buckingham Palace to St Paul's, cramming every foot of pavement, every window and rooftop. Hundreds of them had slept out on the pavements. For the first time in Britain police stationed along the route faced outwards, watching the crowd. But despite advance fears of trouble, there were no incidents – only a spirit of carnival in which the police themselves joined. Red, white and blue were applied to everything – clothes, hats, umbrellas, hair and even faces, and to the periscopes that rose in thickets above the mass of heads. Buses, taxis and even police cars were festooned with red, white and blue ribbons or adorned with the Prince of Wales' feathers.

*　　*　　*

It was a day on which British crowds regained their reputation for gentleness, good humour and fervent patriotism, and were even thanked for their good behaviour by the Metropolitan Police Commissioner.

7

and the Oval cricket ground, she was also losing something. On this coach-journey she took leave of her girlhood. She was saying good-bye to her carefree lifestyle of sharing flats, wearing jeans and sloppy sweaters, nipping about in a Mini Metro, popping into shops to buy things off the peg and on the spur of the moment ... even of giving the photographers who tailed her for so long a friendly wave and a 'Morning, chaps'.

Already she had changed in appearance from the casual look in corduroys and an impudent trilby to the couturiere's client.

At just 20, it seemed a bit soon. No wonder her sideways looks from the corners of her eyes sometimes reminded people of a hunted fawn. Surrounded by protocol and precedent she was going to have to fight hard to keep her sparky attitude to life which had won the approval of the nation.

But for Prince Charles, pausing on the steps of the Cathedral to give the world his last bachelor wave, life was not going to change very much ... except in one enormously important respect. The loneliness would be gone.

He would have someone, other than his parents, who could tell him how things had really gone. He would have someone to laugh with – how she loves to laugh – an instant antidote to the pomposity that surrounds royal occasions. In his manner, earnestness and jokiness contend with each other as his very strong sense of duty struggles with his sense of fun. Fun, one feels, will be gaining a boost from this Princess.

Besides, as he stood on the steps waiting at the church, he was free, at last! Free of all the romantic rumours and gossip and speculation and the attentions of hopeful girls. The right one was just five minutes away.

So he walked into a church brimming with 2,650 wedding guests whose hats and uniforms glowed like flower borders on either side of the long nave.

The Glass Coach drew up and people gasped at the secret of the day, the wedding dress, as it first came into view. The train seemed to go on and on and on as it was unfurled from the coach and billowed behind her, rippling down the red-carpeted steps in a 25-foot ivory cascade.

It was a theatrical dress for which English silkworms had worked over-time. Ivory pure silk taffeta fell from her tiny waist and along the seemingly endless lace-edged train. A romantic ruffled collar set off her bare neck. Like the bodice and the cuffs it was trimmed with delicate, creamy lace.

The whole dress and train were intricately embroidered with 10,000 mother-of-pearl sequins and pearls, and a tiny gold horse-shoe for luck had been stitched among them. The dress designed by David and Elizabeth Emanuel was accompanied by a lace-edged wedding umbrella and delicate ivory silk slippers decorated with 542 mother-of-pearl sequins and 134 pearls with pretty heart-shaped motifs on the toes.

Continued on page 15

FACING PAGE and ABOVE: *Among the guests at the Cathedral were foreign crowned heads (centre left), members of the British Royal Family (bottom left), the weighty King of Tonga and his queen (top left), a smiling Mrs Nancy Reagan (top right) and a serious Mrs Margaret Thatcher (above). The bride's stepmother, Lady Spencer (top centre) wore the cornflower blue which, inspired by the bride's engagement outfit, was a popular choice among the women guests.*

ABOVE RIGHT: *The Queen is greeted at the entrance to St Paul's by the Archbishop of Canterbury, the Most Reverend and Right Honourable Robert Runcie, and the Bishop of London, the Right Reverend Graham Leonard.*

BELOW RIGHT: *The bridegroom's procession forms up at the end of the nave.*

ABOVE LEFT: *The two youngest bridesmaids, Catherine Cameron, aged six, and Clementine Hambro, aged five, delighted every onlooker. With their ruffled dresses, garlanded heads and baskets of meadow flowers, they looked as if they had walked out of a Victorian painting.*

ABOVE RIGHT: *Senior bridesmaid, Lady Sarah Armstrong-Jones, aged 17, won everyone's admiration for the calm competence with which she controlled and steered the bride's seemingly endless train.*

RIGHT: *The bride en route to the church with a commoner's escort of mounted police. The Glass Coach she rode in had carried The Queen to her wedding, as Princess Elizabeth, in 1947 and Princess Anne to hers in 1973. Although known as the Glass Coach because of its large windows, little could be seen of the Lady Diana except a shy smile through a cloud of tulle veil.*

10

ABOVE: *When the dress was finally revealed, the train seemed to go on for ever. Its 25 feet spread out down the whole first flight of the Cathedral steps, as two bridesmaids busily smoothed it out. Meanwhile Earl Spencer, leaning on his assistant's arm, waited to accompany his daughter up to the top, watched anxiously – on account of his recent ill-health – by viewers across the country. In the forecourt of St Paul's Cathedral there was a tri-service guard of honour mounted by the Royal Navy, the Royal Regiment of Wales and the Royal Air Force supported by the band of the Royal Marines. The guard of honour on the steps of the Cathedral was composed of 11 officers from each of the three armed services. Lining the route from Buckingham Palace to St Paul's were some 100 officers and 2,000 men from the Royal Navy, the Army and the Royal Air Force. Twelve bands on the route played throughout the day.*

RIGHT: *Like a beautiful ship under full sail, the bride ascends to the portico, her train streaming in her wake and her veil billowing in the breeze. Seldom has a bride made such a spectacular entrance. Ahead of her, beyond the pillars, the State Trumpeters of the Household Cavalry can be seen, their instruments raised to announce the arrival of the bride with a resounding fanfare.*

11

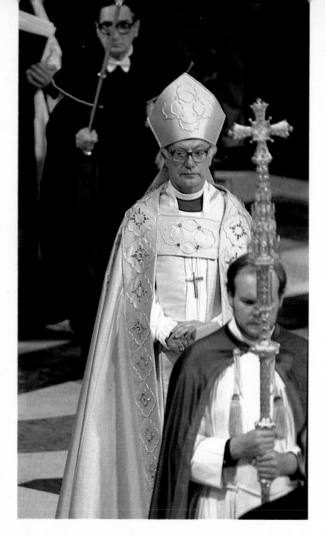

ABOVE LEFT: *Preceded by the Primatial Cross, the Archbishop of Canterbury, Dr Robert Runcie, gleams with silver in a jewelled mitre and cope specially made for the occasion.*

ABOVE RIGHT: *The bride begins her three-and-a-half-minute procession up the aisle, to the music of the Trumpet Voluntary. Beside her on the long journey walks her* *father, Earl Spencer, erect and proud. Ahead of them stretches the longest royal red carpet ever installed, over 650 feet of it.*

BELOW: *The entry of the bridesmaids, in their demure Victorian dresses with yellow sashes. Behind the little ones come India Hicks and Sarah Jane Gaselee, followed by the pages, Lord Nicholas Windsor and Edward van Cutsem. Bringing up the rear* *is Lady Sarah Armstrong-Jones in a full-length version of the dress, carrying a pos*

FACING PAGE: *The bridal procession joins the bridegroom and reaches the platform where the Archbishop is waiting. Ahead of the bride the Dean and Canons of St Paul's, in their copes of scarlet and gold, proceed to their seats in the quire with the Bishop of London.*

There was another show-stopper in the youngest bridesmaids, Clementine Hambro and Catherine Cameron, aged five and six. They followed behind like Victorian country maids dressed in flounced and scallop-edged calf-length dresses of ivory, carrying baskets of meadow flowers, which also garlanded their heads.

They were followed by two other bridesmaids, India Hicks and Sarah Jane Gaselee, and the two pages, Lord Nicholas Windsor and Edward van Cutsem, in the uniform of mid-Victorian naval cadets.

Finally, in a full-length dress came the capable, crisis-averting Lady Sarah Armstrong-Jones. She proved her mettle many times during the service, controlling that awesome train and steering it expertly round corners like a coxswain.

As the bride began her three-and-a-half minute procession up the long aisle, bearing her cascading bouquet before her, every woman's head turned to take in a triumph of romantic drama.

Ahead of her proceeded the Archbishop of Canterbury, himself resplendent in a newly made silver cope and mitre, and the Dean and Canons of St Paul's in copes of scarlet and gold. The 'Trumpet Voluntary' by Jeremiah Clarke, organist of St Paul's when Wren's building was just being completed, can scarcely have accompanied a more brilliant procession.

As marriage services go, it was like all others magnified a hundred times. 'Here', said Archbishop Runcie, voicing the thoughts of everyone present or watching, 'is the stuff of which fairy-tales are made' – looking like someone in fairy-tale splendour himself, if fairy-tales had archbishops in them. But, he pointed out, no one lived happily ever after, without trying to create a more loving world than this one, in which many seem to have surrendered to fatalism about cruelty, injustice, poverty, bigotry and war. This was especially true of 'this marriage in which are placed so many hopes'.

Continued on page 27

FACING PAGE, ABOVE: *The Royal Family waiting for the ceremony to begin: The Queen turns round to exchange a word with Captain Mark Phillips.*

FACING PAGE, BELOW: *Two studies of the bridesmaids during the service. Catherine Cameron (right) joins in the prayers.*

RIGHT: *Other members of the Royal Family occupying the front row of the main congregation join in the singing. Above are foreign heads of state.*

ABOVE: *'Forasmuch as Charles Philip Arthur George and Diana Frances have consented together in holy wedlock, and have witnessed the same before God and this company, and thereto have given and pledged their troth either to other, and have declared the same by giving and receiving of a ring, and by joining of hands; I pronounce that they be man and wife together, In the name of the Father, and of the Son, and of the Holy Ghost.'* Now that they are married in the sight of God the Prince and Princess of Wales are about to perform the legal part of the ceremony by signing the register.

THE CENTREFOLD PICTURES

FACING PAGE 16: *The Patrick Lichfield view of the happy newly-weds just returned from the Cathedral.*

FACING PAGE 17: *A close-up of the bride, showing the intricate embroidery on her dress with pearls and mother-of-pearl sequins.*

CENTRE OPENING, LEFT: *Just before the bride sets off up the nave, the dress receives some last-minute adjustments from its young designers, David and Elizabeth Emanuel. On the left is Lt. Col. Sir John Johnston, Comptroller of the Lord Chamberlain's Office, who was responsible for organising the ceremonial and co-ordinating the activities of all authorities connected with the Royal Wedding. In the foreground is the Archbishop of Canterbury.*

CENTRE OPENING, RIGHT: *A romantic study of the new Princess of Wales in the aftermath of a ceremony that Prince Charles called 'a marvellous emotional experience'.*

INSIDE, LEFT: *During the photographic session, which lasted about 45 minutes, the Princess flopped down on the floor, happy but exhausted. Prince Charles bent over her in fun with a grand operatic flourish. As she laughed, Lord Lichfield took the lower picture. They were still laughing when Prince Charles straightened up (above). Looking on, The Queen and the Royal Family were all highly amused.*

INSIDE, CENTRE: *The landau carries the relieved newly-weds back to the Palace.*

INSIDE, RIGHT: *On the Palace balcony, the couple look out at the crowd with some of their bridesmaids and, below, the formal wedding group of the Prince and Princess of Wales surrounded by all their attendants.*

ABOVE: *The Spencer family group shows the likeness between the three sisters. On the left is Lady Jane with her husband, Mr Robert Fellowes, Assistant Private Secretary to The Queen. On the right is* *Lady Sarah with her husband, Mr Neil McCorquodale. Their brother Charles, Viscount Althorp, stands between their mother, the Hon. Mrs Shand Kydd, and grandmother, Ruth, Lady Fermoy.*

BELOW LEFT: *The Choir of the Chapels Royal and the renowned St Paul's choir with their conductor, Barry Rose.*
BELOW: *Mr George Thomas, Speaker of the House of Commons, reads the Lesson.*

LEFT: *At the heart of the ceremony, the Archbishop gives the blessing, placing his hands on the couple's heads.*

FACING PAGE: *As the bridal couple approach the High Altar, the magnificence of Wren's quire is dominated by the baldacchino, based on that in St Peter's, Rome. At the altar can be seen the three other prelates who took part in the ecumenical service: Lord Coggan, former Archbishop of Canterbury, the Moderator of the Church of Scotland, the Rt. Rev. Andrew Doig and Cardinal Basil Hume, Archbishop of Westminster.*

BELOW: *The signatures on the Cathedral Register, 'Charles P' and 'Diana Spencer' below that of 'Robert Cantuar'.*

BELOW LEFT: *During the signing, the Maori opera singer, Kiri Te Kanawa, and The Bach Choir sang Handel's aria 'Let the bright Seraphim': 'Let their celestial concerts all unite Ever to sound his praise in endless morn of light.'*

BELOW RIGHT: *On emerging as Princess of Wales, the bride curtseys to The Queen before beginning her triumphant journey down the aisle.*

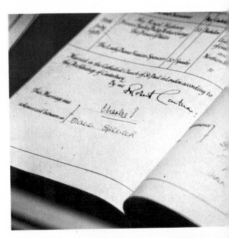

ABOVE: *The moment when the newly-weds first faced the roar of the crowd, outside the West Doors beside the massive pillars of the Cathedral portico. It was a moment to overawe even a prince. As for the bride, she had entered through these pillars a commoner, and now she emerges as the Third Lady of the Realm.*

LEFT: *Returning to the Palace, Clementine Hambro absorbs the sights and sounds in the crowded streets.*

FACING PAGE, ABOVE: *On the Palace balcony both Prince Charles and his father Prince Philip, are delighted by the littlest bridesmaid of all. Clementine Hambro looks over the parapet, stunned for the moment by the deafening reception of the crowd.*

FACING PAGE, RIGHT: *A romantic gesture by the Prince. It was not, however, enough to satisfy the crowd. 'Kiss her!' they called and, for the first time in public, he did – as can be seen on page 1.*

The Royal Wedding Clothes
by Drusilla Beyfus

The delighted worldwide reception given to Lady Diana Spencer's wedding attire confirms that fairy princesses are as popular as ever. The extravagantly romantic figure of the Princess of Wales, the splendidly attired Prince and their courtly young attendants suggests a reversal of the view that it is politic for royalty to appear to be much like the rest of us.

The first point to make about Lady Diana's bridal dress is that it was right in terms of style for the time, the place

and the people. Opinion may vary as to the finer points of execution but the mood that distance lends enchantment, that romance should have its day, was well judged.

The wedding dress and the clothes and effects worn by the bridal attendants combined the familiar with the unexpected, tradition with innovation, the personal with the ceremonial and the young idea with what has been practised for centuries.

Lady Diana Spencer's wedding dress possessed a chaste glamour, and fashion historians will note that it seemed to depart from the recent royal taste for greater simplicity in bridal apparel. It was made by two young British designers, the husband and wife team of David and Elizabeth Emanuel, and gained its inspiration from Victoriana, Edwardian theatre and ballet costume, Arthur Rackham's fairy-tale book illustrations, Tudor influences, all put together in a manner that expressed the wearer's known taste for the romantic.

Lady Diana continued the bridal tradition of folklore by wearing 'something old', a flounce of antique Carrick-ma-Cross lace which belonged to Queen Mary and was employed to form the lace panels on the dress; of 'something borrowed', which was a pair of diamond earrings loaned by the mother of the bride, the Honourable Mrs Shand Kydd; and of choosing 'something blue' said to be a minuscule blue bow stitched into the waistline of the design.

The fabric was of finest feather-weight silk, paper taffeta, in an ivory

shade. This was the colour also worn by The Queen for her own wedding in 1947, but whereas The Queen's dress in her role as Heir Presumptive was highly regal, and in a richly embroidered duchesse satin, Lady Diana chose a fabric which owed more to considerations of fashion.

The whole effect was heightened and dramatized by Lady Diana's wedding veil which in the early stages cocooned her in a haze of tulle sparkling with sequins and pearls. It is notable that she remained fully veiled throughout the

marriage responses whereas Princess Anne, for example, at her own wedding in 1973, wore her veil off the face throughout the ceremony.

The flowers carried by the bride reintroduced the idea of a structured shower bouquet which is one of the achievements of traditional British floristry. The bouquet, by Longmans, was of Mountbatten golden roses, white freesias, lily-of-the-valley, stephanotis, white Odontoglossum orchids and trailing ivy leaves. Traditional myrtle and veronica, both cut from bushes grown from cuttings from Queen Victoria's bouquet, were also included. A similarly important bouquet was part of Elizabeth Emanuel's early wedding dress designs when she was a student at the Royal College of Art.

The young bridesmaids wore dresses that echoed but did not exactly repeat the style of the bride's robe. Identical in colour and atmosphere, each one admitted some variation and difference in order to take account of individual requirements. Hemlines, for example, differed according to the height of the wearer but all showed the ankle. The general effect was of a small troupe of well behaved, beautifully dressed children who had strolled out of the pages of a late Victorian story book illustration. A particularly nice design touch was the use of golden sashes and slippers which introduced a variation on the principal cream tone without breaking out into a completely different colour. The shoes were designed and hand-made by Ivory out of old gold twill. Lady Sarah wore a simple, elegant court shoe with a small heel, while India, Sarah Jane, Catherine and Clementine had pretty flat pumps with a dainty strap.

The attendants' headdresses were crowns of fresh flowers worn on the brow, a new and simplified variation of a line introduced by Paris designers for brides a few years back. The two young pages appeared in Royal Navy cadets' uniforms of 1863, with the white trousers worn during the summer.

Prince Charles as the groom continued the tradition set by Prince Albert at his marriage to Queen Victoria in 1840 when he eschewed the sartorial pageantry of state robes and wore the relative simplicity of service dress. Prince Charles wore full dress uniform as naval commander cut to the instructions of his late great-uncle Earl Mountbatten.

The wider feeling of harmony and unity was reflected in the clothes chosen by members of the two family parties. The group effects contributed to the impression that the individual components had been carefully considered in relation to the whole picture.

The Queen's clothes in turquoise silk crêpe de Chine (made by Ian Thomas) found their complement in the hyacinth blue of the dress worn by the Hon. Mrs Shand Kydd. The Queen Mother's pale green dress (made by John Tullis for Norman Hartnell) was in her favourite fabric of silk georgette. Princess Margaret's fashionable pink and Princess Anne's support for the wedding-day theme of sunshine gold, with Gloucester blue tones and Fermoy sea-green all mingled together without a note of fashion discord. Hats, gloves and handkerchiefs are still *de rigueur* at a royal wedding.

Although the whole occasion has been treated as a superb boost for British fashion design, tailoring and all the allied skills, it would be a pity to imply that the bride and groom were in any way mere clothes horses. Their wardrobe was for real people and served to enhance their individuality.

ABOVE LEFT: *These talented young designers, David and Elizabeth Emanuel of Mayfair, were chosen to design the outfits for the bride and her attendants. They are seen at work in their Brook Street studio. Keeping the dresses a secret was a nightmare and only ten people at the salon were aware of the exact details of the dress. Mrs Nina Missetzis, the seamstress worked in a locked room. A second skirt was made to be sewn over the other in case of any accidental damage.*

Drusilla Beyfus is the internationally famous writer on fashion and author of The Bride's Book *published by Allen Lane.*

ABOVE: *Another Lichfield Wedding Day photograph. Thomas Patrick John Anson, 5th Earl of Lichfield and a cousin of The Queen, first became interested in photography at the age of seven, when he was given a vest-pocket camera. After Harrow he joined the Army in 1957 as an officer cadet, becoming a lieutenant in the Grenadier Guards. During his army career he kept up his interest in photography, and on leaving the service in 1962 he became a professional photographer, despite his* parents' opposition. Within a short time he was working for a number of magazines, including Life and Vogue. *He now combines portraits and fashion with photography for advertising, travelling 200,000 miles a year but still finds time to write.* The Most Beautiful Women *and* Lichfield on Photography *will be published this year.*

Lichfield felt deeply honoured to be invited to take the official wedding photographs, for which he used Hasselblad *and Olympus equipment, with Broncolor lighting. The picture which presented the greatest problem was the large group on pages 28, 29 but he did preparatory research into the height of the subjects in order to plan the composition. The most 'natural' pictures, however, are those not planned beforehand but which capture the light-hearted and joyful mood of the occasion of which there are several in this book.*

25

ABOVE: *Back at the Palace, at last a chance to sit down, surrounded by the swirling river of her train.*

RIGHT: *The five-tiered, five-foot high wedding cake and the Royal Navy Cookery School team from HMS* Pembroke *at Chatham who made it. All two hundredweight and more, it was the responsibility of Lieut. Fred Motley (right), helped by (from left) cooks Dave Avery, David Scott and Ken Fraser.*

It was understandable and reassuring that both bride and groom showed nerves at a ceremony so glaringly lit for public consumption: his 'I will' was foggy and hers was faint. She mixed up his rather cumbersome collection of Christian names, Charles Philip Arthur George, putting the Philip first; he forgot to mention that the goods he was sharing with her were merely 'worldly' goods. None of that mattered. It showed they were human. Relayed to the crowds waiting outside, her every vow was met with cheers of approval.

The ring, which seemed to have been preying on Prince Andrew's mind ever since he had taken charge of it, was safely installed on the bride's finger. It was the last ring to be made from the nugget of gold from a mine in Gwynedd, which had already furnished the wedding rings for the Queen Mother, The Queen, Princess Margaret and Princess Anne. Now there is none left.

There was a new departure in royal weddings in the ecumenical nature of the service. For the first time since the Reformation a scarlet-robed Cardinal, the Archbishop of Westminster, was present. The few words of prayer that Cardinal Hume offered were out of all proportion to the significance of his joining in the service.

There, too, to offer their prayers were the Moderator of the General Assembly of the Church of Scotland,

the Rt. Rev. Andrew Doig, and Prince Charles's Dean and Chaplain at Trinity College, Cambridge, the Rev. Harry Williams. And in splendid musical and dramatic voice was that well-known Methodist lay preacher, the Speaker of the House of Commons. On this occasion Mr George Thomas did not have to call for 'Order, order' in order to send the words of the Thirteenth Chapter of St Paul's First Epistle to the Corinthians ringing down the nave and out into a world where Faith, Hope and Love are sorely needed.

Musically the service was the overwhelming experience that the Prince had planned. There were three choirs and members of three orchestras present, between them requiring four conductors. Two groups of trumpeters sounded fanfares. And the great Father Willis organ of St Paul's thundered over all. The blend rolled round beneath Wren's whispering dome with exhilarating intensity and volume.

In overall musical charge was Sir David Willcocks, the director of the Royal College of Music, who had himself supplied a new version of the much-rearranged National Anthem, with fizzing bursts of side-drums to introduce it and a high, floating descant for the trumpeters in the stratosphere above the last verse.

The music played was British throughout. Specially commissioned

for the service was a setting of Psalm 67 by William Mathias, the Welsh composer, and a set of sung Versicles and Responses by Christopher Dearnley, the organist of St Paul's.

There were several high points: the echoing fanfare from the Whispering Gallery itself, which greeted the return of the bride and groom from signing the register; the Orlando Gibbons 'Amen' dying beautifully away in the quire stalls so richly carved by Grinling Gibbons, two Gibbonses working together to perfection.

Most uplifting of all, the combination of George Frederick Handel, who long ago played the organ in St Paul's, and Sir Christopher Wren, whose soaring Baroque arches and mosaic-encrusted saucer domes blended in an audio-visual experience not to be forgotten, as the Maori opera singer Kiri Te Kanawa sang the aria 'Let the Bright Seraphim'. The glittering sound of high

ABOVE: *The formal wedding photograph of the families of the bride and groom with the bride's attendants: on the left the Windsors and on the right the Spencers. This one is perhaps unique in that everyone is looking at the camera at the right time. The younger bridesmaids and the pages look a little solemn and tired, which is not surprising as several hours have passed since they first assumed their duties.*

27

trumpet and high soprano bounced off the iridescent mosaics of angels with wings of emerald, lapis lazuli and amethyst. This richness seemed to evoke Venice, rather than London EC4.

The hymns were 'I vow to thee, my country', chosen by the bride, and 'Christ is made the sure Foundation' by Henry Purcell, which Prince Charles chose for its 'marvellous, very moving harmonies'. 'I shall probably spend half the time in tears', he had said on television beforehand, and sure enough, he was brushing a tear from his eye after the Amen.

Finally, the bride and groom came down the red-carpeted aisle to Edward Elgar's 'Pomp and Circumstance' March No. 4 in G, smiling in greeting to their friends in the congregation.

Behind them lay the Cathedral register signed 'Charles P' and, for the last time, 'Diana Spencer' beneath the Archbishop's 'Robert Cantuar'.

One-sixth of the world's population was watching on television when they emerged from the long, long nave into the sunshine. She bit her lips and then moistened them as she heard the ocean of cheering begin to break. All the way back to the Palace in the open landau you could see both of them feeling relief and gaining confidence. It was over. Her waves and her smile grew less tentative and shy. By the time they reached the Strand, they could exchange words and smiles shutting out the 600,000 who were shouting themselves hoarse only yards away.

Meanwhile the 12 bells of St Paul's were ringing out the first of the 5,000 changes of Stedman Cinques – a four-hour pull for the 13 ringers who belong, like all city ringers, to the Ancient Society of College Youths dating back to the 17th century. The Poet Laureate, Sir John Betjeman, is fond of bells and their ringers and this explains the couplet in his ode celebrating the wedding:

Come College Youths, release your twelve-voiced power
Concealed within the graceful belfry tower
Till loud as breakers plunging up the shore
The land is drowned in one melodious roar.

Drowned in the melodious roar the parents and relatives emerged from the Cathedral. Both mothers compressed their lips, as mothers do at weddings, looking a little solemn, a little anxious, a little bereft.

The Queen stood aside to allow Earl Spencer, who had been helped down the steps on an usher's arm, climb first into her carriage. But, proud as Punch and just as genial, he was soon waving and smiling more unrestrainedly than she was. Both fathers were relaxed. Prince Philip beamed away at Mrs Shand Kydd in the carriage they shared.

The next appearance was on the balcony of Buckingham Palace, festooned in crimson as it is on these occasions. As the last of the carriages had reached the gates, the crowd flowed down the Mall like a wave behind a dam of linked policemen, circling the Victoria monument and filling every inch of space outside the Palace railings with a sea that also roared melodiously.

Observing the seething ocean of faces outside the Palace gates, an American commentator on the Victoria Memorial at the foot of the Mall, was moved to astonishment. 'Nobody', he said, marvelling, 'trod on the flowers!' It was an observation that summed up the good tempered atmosphere of the day.

The Prince and his new Princess came out on the balcony holding hands, surrounded by their bridesmaids and pages. 'Kiss her!' shouted the crowd, again and again. Prince Charles's lips could be seen forming the question to his bride. The answer was 'Yes'. She turned to him for their first public kiss, which was on the front pages of all the

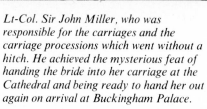

ABOVE, TOP LEFT: *The departure of the newly-weds for their honeymoon through the Palace archway revealed the high-spirited gesture of the Prince's two brothers, Prince Andrew and Prince Edward. His carriage was festooned with blue helium-filled balloons, sporting the Prince of Wales' feathers. When the back of the carriage could be seen (lower left), so could the brothers' hand-written sign, 'JUST MARRIED', adorned with hearts.*

ABOVE, TOP RIGHT: *At Waterloo Station the Princess thanks the Crown Equerry,*

Lt-Col. Sir John Miller, who was responsible for the carriages and the carriage processions which went without a hitch. He achieved the mysterious feat of handing the bride into her carriage at the Cathedral and being ready to hand her out again on arrival at Buckingham Palace.

LOWER RIGHT: *The Prince shakes hands with a British Rail official beside the royal train. The bride's going-away outfit, in pale coral pink with a dashing hat decorated with ostrich feathers, was one of the most ravishing that even she has worn.*

newspapers the next morning. 'You'll Never Walk Alone' sang the crowds in response.

After that, there were as many curtain calls as at Covent Garden, with the pages and the bridesmaids peeping over the parapet stunned by what they saw, as well they might be. Little Clementine Hambro, great-granddaughter of Sir Winston Churchill, quite unselfconsciously sucked her thumb at the world.

One of the two pages, young Edward van Cutsem, was so lost in the spectacle that he did not notice the royal party had gone in and left him gazing there alone. Mrs Shand Kydd brought him back to earth with a sharp tap on the head from a rolled-up programme.

A final roar of appreciation was given for the Queen Mother, who also had stood on this balcony on her own wedding day as long ago as 1923.

Then they went indoors for a well-earned wedding breakfast with 120 family members and guests. The formal family photographs were taken and the wedding cake, five feet high and 225 lbs in weight, was cut to the accompaniment of the usual toasts. It had been made by the Royal Naval Cookery School at Chatham.

This was a small family party, but it had been preceded by a big one. Two nights before, The Queen and Prince Philip had given a dinner in honour of the bride and groom, followed by a large reception for their young friends. Several hundred of them danced into the night to the band of Kenny Ball and his Jazzmen and a pop group, Hot Chocolate.

All this while, the great bulk of the crowd stayed put. They were waiting to see the bride in her going-away dress and when it came it was no disappointment. Now she was Diana the huntress, in an audacious hat, with a saucy turned-up brim decorated with ostrich feathers in a pale shade of coral pink, matching her silk tussore dress and bolero. Round her throat was a choker of pearls. It became her even more than any daytime outfits we had seen so far – and that is saying a great deal.

Just before their going-away landau

ABOVE: *Although the royal couple were gone, the merry-making continued at street parties all over the capital and across the country. But Charles and Diana were together enjoying privacy at last at Broadlands (below), the late Earl Mountbatten's home overlooking the quiet waters of the River Test. There the Prince had his earliest taste of salmon fishing, and there the pair of them could now fish in peace.*

31

left the Palace, Prince Andrew had fixed a hastily written 'JUST MARRIED' notice to the back of it adorned with arrowed hearts and the initials C and D. Prince Charles's two brothers and their friends had also had an absolute inspiration: the carriage pulled away towards Waterloo Station flying a cluster of gas-filled, royal blue and silver balloons with the Prince of Wales' feathers on them. It was their surprise to the newly-weds – more elegant than old shoes but in the same spirit of letting the hair down. The crowds roared with delight.

At the station the royal train was waiting to take them to Romsey, Hampshire, where thousands more well-wishers were patiently awaiting them outside the gates of Broadlands, the late Earl Mountbatten's home.

On the platform the new Princess gave her other public kisses of the day – to Lord Maclean, the Lord Chamber-

ABOVE: *Three days later Prince Charles flew his bride to Gibraltar, where they embarked on the Royal Yacht* Britannia *for a fortnight's honeymoon cruise through the Mediterranean. Its ports of call remained a closely guarded secret. Gibraltar turned out with joy to demonstrate its loyalty to Britain and the crown. An armada of beflagged yachts and motor launches in the harbour gave* Britannia *a royal send-off of ships' hooters and cheers.*

lain, on whose shoulders the organization of the event had rested and his deputy, Sir John Johnston. They could now relax. There had not been a single detectable hitch.

By six o'clock the gates of Broadlands had closed behind them – and the honeymoon could begin in the most closely guarded privacy available in England.

For the television cameras, the party was over, but in the back streets it was only just beginning. Street parties in roads criss-crossed with Union flags were in full swing in towns and cities across the land. Children were put into fancy dress and crammed with hamburgers and lemonade; bells were rung; pigs were roasted; Morris dances were danced and so were more recent varieties; fountains were jumped into and the toast, of course, everywhere was to the happy couple.

Yes, you could say that it cost a great deal, not only to stage but in lost production. As a nation we had taken a day off from everything bleak and depressing in 1981, a day off from unemployment, inflation, and the Public Sector Borrowing Requirement.

It was, however, a day off that embodied the unity of a nation which had not been much in evidence lately. Because a royal family was celebrating, we became a family again, a happy family where friendliness was the order of the day. It was a piece of magic which

can only be worked by a royal family that has earned its place in their subjects' hearts because they are real, as well as royal.

Perhaps that is why so many hundreds of millions were watching too, spectators of a love story and a family occasion in which the British feel they have a part. Perhaps other nations envy us that.

ACKNOWLEDGEMENTS

Press Association: front cover, pp. 10, (top left, bottom), 16, 26. Rex Features: back cover, pp. 2, 4, 6 (left: top and bottom; right: third and fourth from top), 18 (top right), 19, 20, 21 (top), 30 (right: top and bottom); centrefold pp. iv–v, vi (top). BIPNA: pp. 1, 8 (top centre), 15 (bottom), 20 (bottom), 30 (top left). Picture Power: pp. 3, 6 (right: second from top), 7 (left: top and bottom, bottom right), 11 (bottom), 21 (bottom). Anwar Hussein: pp. 5, 6 (top right), 10 (top right), 30 (bottom left). Illustrated London News Picture Library: pp. 7 (top left), 8 (top: left and right, bottom), 9 (top left), 11 (top), 12 (top left), 14, 15 (top). Patrick Lichfield (Camera Press): pp. 25, 27, 28, centrefold pp. i, iii, vi (bottom), vii, viii. Syndication International: pp. 9 (right: top and bottom), centrefold p. i. Tim Graham: pp. 13, 15 (bottom right), 24. London Newspaper Service (Peter Abbey): pp. 17, 18 (left: top and bottom). Camera Press: pp. 8 (centre left), 12 (top right, bottom). Mary Evans Picture Library: p. 23 (top). Theo Bergström (MBP Marketing & Promotional Services): p. 23 (bottom). Brian Shuel: p. 31 (top). Broadlands (Romsey) Ltd: p. 31 (bottom). Beken of Cowes: p. 32.

The book was designed by R. E. Willson with layouts by Dick Richardson; it was edited by Rachel Stewart and Teresa Francis, with picture research by Elizabeth Wiltshire and John Stidolph.

Printed in Great Britain ISBN 85372 332